New Life Not Death

New Life Not Death

Tame your tongue and speak with love

Toya Terese Stone

iUniverse, Inc.
New York   Bloomington

New Life Not Death

Tame your tongue and speak with love

The views expressed in this work are solely those of the author and do not necessarily reflect the views of the publisher, and the publisher hereby disclaims any responsibility for them.

iUniverse books may be ordered through booksellers or by contacting:

iUniverse
1663 Liberty Drive
Bloomington, IN 47403
www.iuniverse.com
1-800-Authors (1-800-288-4677)

Because of the dynamic nature of the Internet, any Web addresses or links contained in this book may have changed since publication and may no longer be valid.

ISBN: 978-1-4502-0192-6 (sc)
ISBN: 978-1-4502-0196-4 (dj)
ISBN: 978-1-4502-0193-3 (ebk)

Printed in the United States of America

iUniverse rev. date: 1/11/2010

Sex by Nature

Secrets of what my neighbor hath done to me, I care to share.
Quick, give me your ear.
I shall tell you only what the wind doth know as I grow tired.
Night holds hands with the stars as they persuade me into bed.
Moon watches me strip thy body of its material, illuminating my
breast as I sleep.
This moon watches me in my most innocent hours.
Morning skies cried rain in which I stood, but it too corrupted me.
Rain danced down my body, caressing my skin, leaving me wet.
Sun grew jealous and came out to warm me, oh that lovely sun.
Inside I felt hungry so with the persuasion of the honeybee, I with my
lips shared kisses with desire.
This is our secret.
White beauty through the air, a man of feathers, he serenades me
with a song of such flattery.
Wind tickled my side cooling me down, whispering sweet nothings
into my ear.
Green that covers the earth, well served as a pallet from which I had
sex with nature.
The sun set, its rays flirting with my shadow.
Politely, I handed the hungry roots that entangled me my cherry.

Déjà vu

Same pictures and poses.
Candy-complemented holidays in continuous fashion.
Repetitive story to follow a broken heart.
Heroism only defined by death and execution of enemy.
Purple hearts and flowers to say thank you.
A cheap world for sale if anyone conceited enough dares to buy it.
Forgotten streets visited only by the rain, which asks a place to sleep until the sun.
Black and white photographs are easy to look at but not to exist in.
Books are only opened if the title reads nice.
Politely though, I forgive, due to an introduction of the already acquainted.
Hope and all my maybes have been purposely given to a soul who is the color to my black and white.
Vindication.
Who dreams to define heroism by being the saint of skies.
This soul is my woosaw.

Alphabet

Abyss of silence
Breaks my mind
Chaos images I do find
Drug me not into submission
Enlighten my soul in dark noisome prison
Free me now and let me fly
Great cuts pour out blood, oh I die
Hell will not forsake this soul
I am pure and fresh as a whole
Jokes and laughter I do hear
Kissing lips are my own conscious fear
Lost and bound, where is home?
Mindless paths leave me alone
Needless to say I found my way
Oh good Satan, you will pay
Pouring blue streams of dreams
Quiet mouth reveals no screams
Righteous oh the Lord was to me
Silent abyss allowed me to flee
Trenches filled my mouth with dirt
Undefined objects cut my skin; it hurt
Ferocious hands reached at my eyes
Wicked demons failed; I will not die
Xylem to the world of nature
Yearning to take my soulful wager
Zest to the savior of life

Anger

Why does anger approach us all?
It is a stupid, pitiless emotion to feel.
Stupid anger, I gave in to it.
Anger is hell, and I hate it.
Let me be the broken glass, and dare not let me be swept up off the floor.
Hell and hate, hate and hell.
To give in is to fail this test of useless scores.
Not with me will you win.
I stand alone, and alone you feel.

Antique

Be ever so quiet, your voice rages out loud. You see I am trying but
inside I am dying.
Old dust sits and then gathers upon me like an antique.
Just take me home and you can leave me there.
Here I will make friends with the shadows and gossip about all the
cents I am worth.
I am neither a stage nor a director, so quit auditioning and kill the acting.
See, if you were a bee you would care too much about your honey.
Are you blind? Have you lost your eyes? It is pouring. It is not sunny.
Take your shoes off and run in the grass, get a little dirty. Okay, I give up.
Where are you hiding? Fake linens; please just let me rip them.
Can I revive your face because it looks like it is drowning? Don't
crack now, be strong not weak.
Do not bury yourself deep, die an antique. Be the story, not just the title.
I will not laugh at what most people find funny.
Step with me outside as it rains so no one can tell we are crying.
Instead of taking a step, please start to leap, and retire as a noble and
beautiful antique.

Anxiety

I no longer rest in a bed of comfort but instead dwell against the cold cement where neighbors of deep cracks nest. Just a simple walk I took on this pleasant day while my tired mind continues to fail in making me smile.

Coffee shops with dark windows no longer send an invite for a full cup of sweet aroma but a fear of what the people inside can see and I cannot.

Blue skies no longer linger too high for me touch or to get lost in but now fly too low and too dark for me to be found.

A part in life where one can exist as an image is quite popular, but I exist as only a cold wind.

Cold sweats soon start to condensate with the rapid, shallow breathing my mouth pushes forward. Which in my mind creates a fog across the window, while my fear slowly writes, "I have anxiety," for everyone to see.

I dwell in an empty soul where I struggle to love and stay sane, but I fall into an empty soul of fear where I'm learning how to not care and to hate.

Outside is cold, yet I need not the heat of warmth but to just freeze. On solid ground I stare and wonder if it is easier to live as if you're dying or to just die with your last thoughts containing the emotion of not wanting to die but to live.

To be scared is a comfort and happiness to me, but I know the reality of this is supposed to be uncomfortable. In time one shall heal, but like a soul one shall never have full control.

My soul cries when I do, and if I was to rip my soul from my body and lay it in the crack that nest as my neighbor, I would lie there dumb.

I'm without love and those who hold my hand, whose warmth makes me, want to never let go; I manage to yet again be judged by the hidden faces of those who hold a full cup.

In the dirt that covers the earth, that has felt my every step, my prints and travel and my story would be soon forgotten. I do not walk in my own shoes, but I walk barefoot.

In no more comfort do I rest, but on cement where I gaze one last time through the alleys, up the buildings, and at the dark window.

A deep crack, just big enough for me to fall in, would be tempting.

This is where and when one falls, whose identity is controlled by a simple anxiety. In time I hope I heal, but as of now I'm standing on cement on the edge of a crack.

Oddly enough, I shall step forward and fall. Then the cycle shall break, if someone would only catch me.

Atonement

Eyes do not take me seriously; have you forgotten your smile?

They stole you while you were sleeping, and I know it's not fair.

Rage out and scream, run wild, naked, across these fields, and let the sun along with the shadow paint you into the soil.

There I am sure no one can find you. When the rain falls it will cover your tears.

Okay, I will lie next to you and let the earth consume and swallow us whole.

In case you change your mind, I will give God a shovel.

Dig you back up and maybe then you will smile. Two shovels in fact, since I lie here with you.

The days will be cool from the October breeze, and the spring blooms will dress us in colorful attire.

Sweet this life is here next to you, but soon I pray that you ask him to bring his shovel.

I cry because I will miss you; no longer can I lay here with you for the heavens call my name to smile here about the soil.

Your arms are like roots now so confined to this earth.

I love you, friend, and I pray you do not fade.

You are but an oak tree.

There I saw your smile today. I planted a seed in hopes that it will visit you in a while.

August

My heart lies cold on the ground as the snow does in the winter
Harsh winds rock the branches to sleep as my own lie awake and numb
Night fades away and with it my eyelids slowly fall to rest upon my face
Before my soul hibernates, I thank the moon for leaving a light on
In time my neighbor visits and with him he brings the sun
Now my heart grows warm and my tears of snow melt away
Here beside me the sun naps and all of my limbs start to unthaw
Hibernation is now slept away, and with the hot air I stretch myself
awake, and I whisper…
Good morning, my sweet season of August

Battle

Slash my skin from side to side
Leave me broken and here to die
Your eyes are mysterious
The eyes you look with leave me delirious
Our swords pierce the air
Invitations let you step inside my lair
Hymns our motions cried
To our promised creed we lied
Soil changed from brown to red
Rotting corpses made a bed
My shield is cracked
Your sword and my flesh now made a pact
Slash my skin from side to side
Leave me broken and here to die
This is our battle, and so it shall be
When you die, I will be free

Born

Breathe with me, world
Give to the soil a seed
Rise from the ground, a new life
Let the earth hand to the world
Me
Down from the sky, let sins soak into unforgotten elements
Rapture the wind to bring in a new season
Carve your identity into the roots of me
The essence of immortality
I am spoken for

Boy Met Girl

A boy met a girl who was sweet with a smile
A girl met a boy who was simple in this world
She was color and he was black and white
A boy loved the cold
A girl loved the warmth
He was the hunter and full with adventure
She was the poet and complete with a picture
A boy moved to a northern state
A girl continued in a southern state
He became a hero in the plumber world
She became a hero in the disabled world
A boy missed a certain girl
A girl didn't mind this missing her
To heaven this boy's brother went
Home to comfort a friend this girl went
A boy went to Costa Rica
A girl went too and became a step closer
Engaged the two became
Married months later and her name became his name
A boy to become a hero in the world of law
A girl to become a hero in the world of love
She wrote this poem for a simple boy so he could understand
To remember how the two became one, and now I can say
Once upon a time …

Cherry Tree

Underneath the cherry tree
A place where contentment is to be free
You can be you, I can be me
To be unaware, naïve, is considered a good thing
Hearts are in hands as hands are held out, fingers spread open
On purpose
No prices or sale signs

Underneath the cherry tree
Screams of anger do not make you crazy
Here arms are capable of only hugging
Little bluebirds sing in a cappella
Good habits are to sing along

Underneath the cherry tree
There are no yield signs nor live with caution gestures
Canvas; all this that I see is painted by artists
Who are survivors of broken hearts, newfound faith, and stupidity?
Wisdom that makes up for it
Gravity only sits next to what is forgotten
P.S., forgiveness, serenity, righteous reds
The rest goes up

Underneath the cherry tree
Politely a stream enlightens me
I float in this stream of make believe
More like I drown

If you are sad come sit with me, downtown, near the street
Underneath the cherry tree

Chocolate-Covered Poet

In the fall, I imagine me naked, wearing only her colors
With the night I allow the dreams to play with my imagination
I visit enchanted forests where the moon meets the pond
In love I am complete, for without it I would bleed
Enchanted tales are to be written, and like a play, my soul is the words
This mind becomes the author and this heart a simple editor
I believe in Shakespeare and date Poe from time to time
Chocolate is sweet and what I have secret affairs with
A pirate I would enjoy to be, to follow a treasure, to scream aye, mate
I respect the relationship between knowledge and wisdom
The only song I know best is the one complete with laughter
I would like to sleep in a strawberry patch in the middle of summer
Stubborn kisses I give passionately without hesitation and some
would claim
Him to be my best friend
Hungry I am inside to create a war on poverty and neglected innocence
Who I am, I give all thanks to a God who designed me with all these
things
And with the heart to be a poet.

Armadillo

We are never content in life, we always want more.
Our nature is to question life so much that life ignores us and then
we react in anger.
Sometimes in life we love so much and receive no love in return.
Our returns involve excuses, apologies, and all we can do when we are at
our saddest is to quietly nod. To pretend the tears aren't real, not visible.
Inside us we are burning and yearning to say so much.
There is a reminder that pain is only everlasting when
You begin to stop choosing to see the little things in this world that
are still innocent.
Tonight, mine was a hungry armadillo.
Our words are too busy soothing our heart, and no words are
available for our tongue and lips.
There are moments in life that take away such pain, and these
moments may not last for long
But even a second makes a difference.
They help us realize that this sadness doesn't have the power
To consume our every waking thought or process in these moments
hope is accompanied by chance.

Clock Watch Love

I was a fool, failed to see
All the true love he had for me
I realized my love in time
The sounds of a hand in watch rhymed
Sometimes I wonder if I reacted too late
Did take his love as granted fate?
I realized my love in time
The sounds of a hand in a watch rhymed
I regret not returning the love
Now a darkened cloud floats above
I realized my love in time
The sounds of a hand in a watch rhymed
His love for me is real
He understands how I feel
I realized my love in time
The sounds of a hand in a watch rhyme
I feel so apart from him and what we had
Now my soul can't stop weeping, I'm so sad
I realized my love in time
The sounds of a hand in watched rhyme
How times with us are hard
He is strong; he is my guard
I realized my love in time
The sounds of a hand in a watched rhyme
These true emotions do rapture me as a whole
My loving heart joins my fornicating soul
I realized my love in time
The sounds of hand in a watch rhyme
Someday soon we will intertwine
The love I felt lost to, will be mine
I realized my love in time
The sounds of a hand in a watched rhyme
Open gates will creak on by

My heart with his will speak no lies
I realized my love in time
The sounds of a hand in a watch rhymed
My once emotions of unsure love are broken
My strong voice has spoken
I realized my love in time
The sounds of a hand in a watch rhyme
With his ever-unique soul, I'm tied
I now have love to abide
I realized my love in time
This clock watch love did tick with a rhyme

Cloud Nine

I lie to rest now
To dream
So many dreams one can create
Millions hope
To dream is my way to cope
A life without dreams is only nightmares
Closed eyes, a shield
A shield that blocks the universe to leave you as a second ruler
What a dream
So many dreams
My world lies asleep
Cloud nine
Location, a fantasy of survival

Comida Amarilla

Yellow in color I lie with the community of mountains
In sight of me so long a human sweats
Awake the bluebird sings a song of birth, a cue
For me to stretch arms high
Neighbor to the solar system
Skies cover my eyes in fear I might stay too long
I am needed, ironically, to overstay my welcome
Humans search for shade
Jack Frost cares not too much for my appearance
Though my absence alerts the planet
Anticipation is conceived, for we have growth in common
Photosynthesis calls me by name

Comparisons

Sometimes I lie here at night, and I think about how I can relate you to all the things I love in the world. Piece by piece, I remove all the rules, politics, maturity, responsibility, and government from our relationship. Then I slowly take what is left—the deep core of my affection for you—and I use it. Like gift wrap, wrapping all the things in life I consider presents.

Sweet candy comes into thought. Joy and comfort from a simple piece of candy, bring back the memory of a child with no worries, slowly letting the sweetness cover its tongue. The smell of liquorices evades my nose with each lick. Your smile is just like sweet candy, brings a smile to my face, and it adds a flavor to my heart that it loves to taste. The smell of deodorant and old cologne parade my nose with each movement of your body.

Hot showers, your touch, they are identical. A relaxing remedy to all stress.

New Zealand, France, and Ireland. Dream destinations. For now, my head on your chest, your fingers through my hair, arms caressing my bare skin, and the heat of you through your clothes. This is a dream destination come true. It's a place I like to call "You."

Coffee shops, a place where I can daydream in the mist of mocha scents and creamer. A hand holding a cup, a deep breath in reminds me of your satisfying love. You're like my little coffee bean, all brewed up in a cup, and my palms are wrapped tight around its body, feeling warmth, and embracing the richness of a new coffee flavor. Morning refreshment—just like seeing you after it has been a while.

Chocolate—an enjoyment so great, it's almost a sin. Explosions of milk chocolate on my tongue such a taste, alas; mmm, just like your kiss.

A blank piece of paper and a pen. A great utensil and a great place to write a poem. This poem for you.

Braille, a unique type of writing that can help the blind to see. Your soft skin, silk-like chest hair, perfect curves, and shapes. Your five o' clock shadow growing like an open seed; the cracks on your bottom lip; and the blisters on your hand. These all create a wonderful alphabet. You're my Braille when your love blinds me. I love to read your words.

Sunsets are gorgeous. The earth can take a deep breath in; a day is over now, and it can rest. All can sleep. Our goodnight prayers are my sunset. My permission to rest.

Rain, a nurture to nature. Just like the drops, your words fall down upon me and give my eyes a reason to smile.

Books are a story. A place to let your mind run and imagine living in somewhere else. Like a dream. Our book is called "Our Future," full of dreams.

Sunrise. Bright and happy. Like your smile, and a few morning text messages. Little bluebirds chirping to our song.

Sweet nothings; whispers in my ear as I sleep. Little secrets for just you and me.

Alas, a love and a resurrection proved by our Lord. A gift of unconditional love. A pleasant pleasure, a tiny love note, and a new breath no one can take away as long as we speak the truth in front of *Him*.

Ocean, full of color and life. Just like your eyes, blue and green like the seas. Full of life underneath them.

Thunderstorms bold and brave. Like a soldier; like you.

Hot cocoa in the winter, a time of relaxation and Christmastide. You're the angel on my tree, and the present underneath. The cocoa to keep me from feeling cold.

The first fall wind brings a love so softly and a new adventure. Me and you. Just like the words, "I love you."

Peanut butter sandwiches, quilts, brand new flip-flops, favorite pair of jeans, lip gloss, perfect shirt, butterflies, meadows of spring, fall leaves, first bike ride, puppies, church, music—I could go on forever comparing you until I had nothing left to compare. That is why I just say that you're my world. My simple little pleasure.

God be with us, and forgive us, as a mother does her child.

Confused

I feel like crying today
I feel like my words haven't changed
It's amazing how life went from real to fake
It skips, it turns, and then it burns
How are we supposed to learn from the temptations of hell?
Are they to make us stronger or bring us down?
Is this where faith comes around?
I can always ask questions but never get answers
Maybe I should run or try to escape
I want to find love again but all I find is hate

Conspiracy

I know what you don't know
I see what you cannot see
You see what I know
You can't see what I don't know
You're reading my words
Words I wrote
You can see what I know
You read what I wrote
What I know that you don't know is that you can't see what I don't know
Why?
These words I write are what I know
The thing is we both know
What we see and that which we both don't know

Crisis Identity

My mind is pacing now
Hidden images and quiet words pinch at me
I can't think anymore
What happened?
Abyss has risen and clouded my thoughts
I don't remember anything
My body ripples with panic
Earth and its ground under my feet, I don't feel
A luscious red soaks the ground and its soil
A silhouette of a man so dark lies to the side of me
Life no longer breathes through this man
Where am I, and why do I feel guilt creeping upon my hands?
Why is fear caressing my soul?
Has crime yelled my name with a guilty tone, or am I that silhouette
of a man?

Crying Masquerade

I cry here.
My tears are a masquerade dressed in lovely emotions on the ballroom floor.
"Cry with me," the world asks.
"Cry with me on this floor."
"Cry with me until the clock strives twelve."
I accepted the offer.
The clock strikes twelve.
Crying seemed to have such a musical atmosphere.
What a masquerade.

Dancing in Hell

Do not worry.
I will tell your secrets and you will never persuade me.
I will never be like you.
I see the hills on which you stand.
They are not far from mine.
So let's battle; do compete with me.
For the truth of all things, your efforts are weak, pointless.
At the end of time you will be forgotten.
So why do you keep trying to kidnap these souls?
Have you forgotten about the hand that put you here?
Moron, you're uglier than I thought.
Termination is your fate.
So let's dance, my dark friend, and do not step on my feet.

Judge

Woman, why do you keep looking behind you? Answers are not there for the questions you have nursed.

Turn back around and listen. All of what you were dies as the genocide you create inside yourself takes movement. Pain will be slow, and pillows will become better than chocolate.

Yes, time is still moving.

Not everything is exactly still. Constitutions you have written on the stone of your soul, you forgot.

Take your medicine to help you sleep; how much did you pay for those tears?

Can you afford to have them refilled?

No, memories are not your punishment, just reminders of change and strength.

You cannot swim, so why jump into that pool of sorrow?

Sweet, you say; that was his character?

Calm to touch. I am sorry.

This is the price you pay for conviction.

Decision

When we get down on our knees
Hold hand in hand
As we lift our eyes to heaven's land
We pray
Lord, I know in time
We will be all the things we prayed not to be
People will cry and our tongues will lie
We will witness what we good people fear
The time when heaven and hell grow near
There will be a time when all darkness will fall
The cries of humans will crawl
Those who can speak the truth will remain in shadows for the unfair
can see
Will kiss a person of sorrow
This is when hell will come to reclaim
This is when heaven's army will sing
We are taught of good and bad
We thought we knew which land we had
So now I say that now and here
I chose, I stand, and I promise
To stand next to you forever

Element

I creep through the green hair that hangs from the brown arms of the old tree
I make my way down to the ground
I slither through the painted meadow of flowers
I fly fast, visiting nature and never resting upon the solid objects of earth
My touch can turn from cold to hot
I spin, carrying rotted leaves and tumbleweeds across the old wagon trails
I come in contact with people, and I whisper to them all the knowledge I have learned
From far places that I observed
I can feel the souls of people as I play through their hair and shoot up against their bodies
I am a spy to all inner emotions
I can see and feel what not even its master can
I know your secrets, and I know the touch of all nature that you love
I make love to your heart
And I open your soul and whisper to you the many wonders of the sheltered paradise in which you live
I watch you open your arms, hoping that I could stop for one moment and become invisible to your vision
I am your best friend and you know I exist, you just can't see me
You just have to open your soul and hear me
Feel me
My home is outside among the elements, which I call family
My siblings are fire, earth, water
And I am the wind

End Not

I feel so weak and I sense heaven's betrayal settling upon my image
I'm beaten and battered to an extent that the shadows of hell seem
promising
The imprint of my footsteps upon the gardens seems to welcome weeds
White cages no longer are steel with attached locks but instead are
just rusted elements
The makeup and paint that cover my face form a mask of outer illusions
Glory only rises to an extent now, and I'm too short to reach the top
Broken limbs I'm attached to, but solid faith I inhabit, for I still
breathe

Eternity

Closed realms my heart envisioned
Images with emotion my eyes did imprison
A scene enclosed in hands
A flower bloomed on fornicating land
Shadows of ballet move across the wall
Moving so quickly, Thou shall not fall
Evil fills the weak
Glory fights and climbs a peak
Humble hymns we sing
Those happenings lay sheltered under my wing

Fantasy

I am trapped
Set me free
Hold me no longer, let me be
Scream within
Angry shadows roam this silent den
My cheeks are dry from my tears
Closed in space; hello, fears
Cages, I hate cages
Healthy and love I do feel
Entrapment, help me deal
I dream of fantasies
Candy-coated mountains
Lands so green
Blue rivers and streams
There I want to be
My magic kingdom
I am free

Far From

Crying isn't easy anymore, and my eyes would normally be flowing with tears creating a burgeoning wall of wet. And now they parch. Four panes enclose this window, and I have all the details of the cherrywood pane imbedded in my head. Outside this window is an image of fairylands and hobbits. It's here in the distance where I can daydream, just escape.

The world gives a hard beating, but when you can find a place to inhabit outside of reality, then you know that the world has just taken your last dignity. I'm afraid to move my eyes from the castles in the window, and I'm afraid for my soul to create a sheet of blindness to the cherrywood.

There's always those in life who are greater and who can create such a better fantasy, beyond any dimension. This life has left cuts in my heart; the amount of judgment I have enforced upon anyone has left my mind to die, and giving up was instant death.

Now I know what I didn't before and my fantasy is slowly fading. Tears stain the cherrywood.

Fault

Nothing in life is empirical anymore; there is no absolute.
Darkness has become the leading official in the war between my
physical realm and emotional realm.
Simplicity has been traded out for anxiety.
Even my eyes are sad, and I try to keep them from resting upon my face.
Throw me in a prison, a dark hole, and let me rot.
Strength is my definition for love, and even that has been stolen or
consumed by a mouth that preached pure blasphemy.
Swam a million waves of sea to save you from drowning, and it is
almost as if on purpose you looked at me and then swam to the
bottom and slept.
Rescue is why I came.
Stop.
Nothing is empirical anymore; you defined love for me and then
sold your definition for the price of weakness and logic. Stillness
consumes me, and my heart asks where you are.
Never again; and as the sun rises, I will stand in front of it and stare it
in the face and then ask for the moon instead.

Parable

He is a mustard seed
Small in size including shape
Planted amongst the more strong seed in size and shape
The harvest must have a great laugh at the sprouts he hoped to grow
He is a mustard seed
In the womb to which the farmer planted him
He wept with the season rains
Neighboring vegetation discouraged him so
He is a mustard seed
With the sun that his planter promised he sprouted
He rejoiced with the soil that kept him rich inside
The largest in size the mustard seed stood firm
I am a mustard seed
Large in size including shape
Now the king of harvest where the blue birds rest and sing a song
The farmer opens his planting pack
To plant a mustard seed

Take It All Back

Blood from your feet, hands, and side
A man dies slowly for your cries
Leagues of angels he left uncalled
For your freedom, this man took it all

Forgive; 'cause to this world, your blood was not enough
I guess these people think they're tough
Everything and everyone stares with blind eyes
To this world of flesh, I pray another sin does die

Aching hearts want to scream for you
Yet murder, abuse, robbery, and killers are let loose
A pain inside grows so cold; makes me angry, what can I do
Take it all back. Take it all back. Take it all back. Take it all back.

Blood-stained hill just wasn't enough
Neither was that cross you carried for us
What can I do, to make these people love you?
Can't I take it all back, take it all back?

Father, I forgive them for you
Father, I forgive them for you
Father, I forgive them for you
Amen!

Fragile in Disguise

I couldn't move him from the dark space
His eyes wouldn't shine toward the heavens
He was untouchable
When you spoke to him, you would have to whisper
Fragile in disguise he was
Limp his arms seemed to be
Just a cold rock floor covered with dust of ages surrounded him
I tried to search for a switch to make light visible
I could only stare and imagine what emotion inhabited him
He was dead but alive in so many ways
Fragile in disguise he was

Freedom Isn't Free

I woke up this morning, and each day since you have been gone, I find the tears a little harder to fall at all.

Maybe it's because I have realized that each new morning is a day closer to your arrival in fall, or maybe it's because I realized that you would rather see my smile most of all.

So later on in the day as the sun began to slip away, I went to our closet and pulled out a pair of your old combat boots and brown undershirts. I'm sure the ones you're wearing now are a lot more covered with sand and dirt.

Your favorite old running shoes are gone now, I'm sad to say. The soles were torn; I had to throw them away.

As I did so, I couldn't help but smile at the memory of you lacing them up and running out the door to PT for a while.

You would never leave without a kiss on the cheek, a kiss so sweet. I looked across the bed and imagined you there, kneeling on your knees with me, and saying our prayers with care.

I was going to write you another letter, but I thought of something better. With my head bowed, I said out loud, "Dear God, send him a post card with a lot of love, and send him faith from up above. Seal it with your hope, well wishes, and a few of my kisses."

Before I finished, God and I made up a care package, nice and furnished.

This one is a little too big to send in the mail, but if you close your eyes you will see that we sent you an angel.

Glory Corpse

Present to me a riddle to guess
Let my intelligence grow less
Cut my finger for it points
Whack my arm from joint to joint
Let the sky rise and speak
The sun shall shine to its ozone peak
Abyss and blindness to me prevail
Unwanted emotions rise from hell
Poke and torture my dirty skin
I cannot fight back; I am weak within
O glory God, send down your wind
My heart is stiff; let it bend
Inside, my mind is gone
Let your verses make me strong
Teach me home above all laws
Out into the world I will crawl
My world is not a Holocaust
My bones and flesh shall not be lost
Ceremony within me dances
I have found my lost chances

God

The night shines through my window
My eyes are now closed as I place my hands together
I whisper silently these words to myself and to you
Lord, I pray that you befriend those who are strangers to your love
Lord, I pray that you give shelter to those not yet at home in your
caring arms
I pray that you feed those who are hungry for your faith, Lord
Sometimes I wonder what the night would be like without the stars
I always think how pretty the leaves are in the fall
Then I frown because all the beauty is fading
People are forgetting who they are and where they should be
My fears subside now that you've answered my prayers
I recall that you said to me in silent ways
To say hello to unfamiliar faces
To feed those who ask for food
To keep those warm that live in the cold
Then you'll see that your prayers have been answered

Gone

He is gone now
I'm thinking of so many ways to change his mind
I miss him so
My tears sting my face
With him he took a part of my soul
Now I'm afraid I will never be whole
At times I wish he'd die
My heart hates him so
Although I feel this way
I still feel love for him
The hardest thing is saying goodbye
Facing reality of broken love
He is happy
(I know deep down that he is not)
I dare not ask him to show what he does not want to
This love is over; I surrender
I fear love now
I wonder if I could live with my fragmented soul
In order to survive I smile at our memories
I walk away, knowing that love might be a fear
This fear is not presented in the dark
So goodbye, my first love
Farewell

Good and Hate

The gravitational pull of faith.
The gravitational pull of hate.
The pain within the heart.
The crying soul within a tear.
They cry of help.
The wound of courage.
The eyes to see.
The mind to speak.
The brain to think.
The tongue to taste.
The words to understand.
The love to fulfill.
The gravitational pull of faith, the cause.
The gravitational pull of hate, the effect.

Goodbye, Kane

Lost my soul
Bloodied mind still whole
A murderer you are
Escaped convict, you ran too far
I laugh at you
Lost, now what to do?
Keep running, you coward
I will find you; you will be overpowered
Forgot to cover your tracks
Easy giveaway, don't leave facts
Now where are you, you awful ghost?
What soul will you now host?
Invisible you are not
I should kill you, let you rot
Look at these faces
You strangled their necks with laces
They were crying; could you not hear?
Of course, drowned you were with fear
Guilty acts you created
Your soul of evil will be jaded
Goodbye, you darkened whole
Strangled now, is your soul

Grandbabies

You're still in your place where I always envisioned you
Even though your appearance is invisible, you are there
But my image of you will always be to my heart, true
I can still see you in my mind; my soul feels fair
What made you smile I do not know, but I always liked to feel as if I
had a clue
You are gone now, papa, and I wish I could reach to the heavens and
take you back
I miss you, like a dark abyss misses its light, I feel so blue
Your essence to my soul I do lack
I did shed tears for you; I think I might even have watered the ground
But my tears on the ground soaked the earth in which you were sleeping
Now I only smile, for you are in my heart; you are found
A pariah no longer to my feelings, my soul has stopped weeping
I walk this earth now in happy joy that you are walking behind me
Neither more sadness nor guilt; I love you, and your grandbabies are free

Halloween

As the sun goes to sleep
I will rise with the moon
Gather at these tombs and sing a song for the living
We will be the haunting
Winter wind will scream with excitement as the sleepy willow dances
in sorrow
Dark angels stop to see all the commotion in this cemetery
Ravens fly with speed as this night comes to be
A celebration for the living
Ghosts kiss to the lighter times, ones we all remember
Skeletons will ask the night to dance
The moon's stomach will grow large as he snacks on the night
Here is to the living with all our haunting sweetness
You're what we are no longer but we sing so not to not fear us
Hum hum hum
Hum hum hum to the ones who sleep in life
A haunting lullaby
We will be the haunting who sing
To the living!

Heaven

I take this time to let go and fly.
This time I'm free.
I fly over every hidden aspect that I was blind to.
No more can hurt and agony caress my soul.
It's beautiful up here.
The wind never felt as cool.
This dimension is by far the most precious place and dream.
Here I can see what I never knew.
I can see what people tried to show me my whole life.
I'm just free now.
Tears fall from my eyes to the soil.
That is where my knowledge will grow.

Dear Heavenly Father,

Today was a good day, a quiet day, but you still threw in a little good food, smiles, love, and a lot of rest. I was watching television tonight and saw a couple of kids too poor to have surgeries that were very much needed, and I saw women selling their bodies for some money because they weren't as fortunate as I. Things like that, Father, they're horrible. Some people just start not to care anymore when their lives become nothing in their eyes, and it's then that they begin to believe that you don't exist. Life is what you make it. People spend so much of their time trying to find somebody or something to blame for what they have become. It doesn't make us pathetic; it makes us weak; weak enough to where running away from the truth just gets harder. The truth is something all of us want to deny, that's why half us are really great liars. Father, you're supposed to keep us safe, keep us from hurting; I mean, you're God, so why do you take away those we love? Why do you allow us to go broke or get terminally sick? We ask you that every day, don't we? Mom always said that things happen for a reason, and I believe she is right. See, what I've learned and what I've read: you really love us. But you don't live our lives for us, and you can't help somebody if somebody doesn't want to believe in you. Some people fail to remember that evil is out there too. You believe in us so much, we just find it hard to believe you exist; but that's part of the problem too: we don't want to believe that just maybe something that we were taught exists, doesn't. If believing is so hard, then why do we use the word? You teach us morals to follow; these are the morals to keep us from becoming thieves, which can lead to us losing our jobs; to keep us from having affairs, which can lead to your wife or husband leaving you; you teach us to love our enemies, which could prevent wars; and to keep us from being greedy and to share, so that maybe people wouldn't be starving. Life isn't made to be a field trip; it's made to teach us. That maybe if your son died or daughter, it's because you, Father, wanted to teach them to get back up on their feet and keep on. You don't want us to rot in misery; you're only trying to make us strong so that our weaknesses won't kill us. Everyone is a soldier.

My heart has been broken, and my life hasn't been like a peach, but I got back up—because I knew I had to set an example to others that when life gets you down you have to get back up, to live for those you have lost, and to rebuild what has fallen down. Death is death; we shouldn't fear it, should we Father? I would rather die proud and in love, than die with sorrow. So thank you, Father, because without you, I wouldn't have figured all this out. And maybe I'm wrong, but I have a few scratches, and my memories are a lifelong lesson. We shouldn't hate you; you said you would love and keep us going at all times, and that is what you do. You never said we wouldn't hurt. If you didn't love us, you wouldn't place a future ahead of us to allow us to keep going. Life hurts; no one ever said it would be easy. Don't look toward the past; see today and wait for tomorrow; isn't that what you said, Father? If you were so hateful, you wouldn't forgive us. So I close my eyes and I pray tonight for those who only believe in themselves. Forgive me for my sins, Father, and forgive those who do not know what they do. Jesus, help us carry our crosses when we become too weak, and let us rejoice in your father. Thank you for all, Father; may you continue to bless us all. Amen.

Hollywood

If you're looking for evidence, then you will find it under my
fingernails, in plain view here on my cheek; here in my black and
white world it will be hard to find the red of blood.
See, cough cough, I removed the door, so just let yourself in; wrap my
floors and walls in your yellow tape, the caution words; well, in my
blind world we can't read, so cuff me for trespassing.
I am raw, dirty; I am broken. I have habits, no nails and sore lips, but
I swear my tongue is clean and my smile is pure.
Glue will do no good to piece me; I have swallowed it all to keep my
organs and heart together.
I am a match, swimming in gasoline; that is how it happened, here in
my black and white world.
This is my goodbye; sorry if the napkin is sticky—pancakes for breakfast.
In your pocket, that is me, my ashes, but not dust to dust; that's an insult.

Home

I rest now upon these mountains
Even though my body has died
I can still feel the breeze cutting at my lips
Stinging the chapped part of my mouth
This pain did not hurt but only made me feel good
It was home
My home to the fenced-in meadows
Meadows that sprang up every spring with
Every color imaginable
Nature painted this picture
But I stole that paintbrush a long time ago
Dancing on the soil, the wet soil after the rain
Descended from the skies
The aroma filled my lungs
Oxygen so pure
I miss home
I am weak no longer
I have died now and I sit here
Not as a passed shadow
But as one that lies about my home

Houdini

Not too clear, must I admit
Existence plays an evil trick
Black hats wore by magicians
Pull out white rabbits and charge for commission
Graveyards rest so silent with the night
Listen with obedience yet they sing
Shovel but to set them free
Man whistles his tune with age
Tap his cane on the corner
Dark lens under his brow, a blind man
Selling his Sal
Homeless and hungry
This should be easy
Sticky situation made clean with decision

Me

Vanished, yes, I feel vanished. More than ever now, and no matter how much I look into the past and try to form myself into that existence, I only fail. My years now in which I live are only me contradicting the silhouette of my wishful existence. When I touch familiar objects, my hands feel scarred by the essence of the object.

Years ago the air outside was inviting and now the air screams limits. No matter how much I want to put forward, I get thrown back against my childhood wall of stigmata. Yet when I write, my limits fade, and I can soar. My existence becomes a melting corpse of lust to my pen.

My heart and soul feel like property to the ink that pours from any writing utensil. My soul and heart are prisoners behind the straight blue lines, and my appearance stands in front of the blue lines with a smile at the acid that burns away the blue lines.

So after every poem or paper I write, I become an escaped convict.

My childhood was free, and I was free. Free to the smiles of friend's faces, free to the color of green that lay upon the soil and dirt; I was free. Free to feel the wind wisp at my feet as I stood in the middle of the road and welcomed Christ to dance with me.

Ice Age

It is amazing how you can stand in one spot so long and wonder if you would ever once more step from that spot and if that one location would walk with you through the rest of your life.

Maybe you wouldn't even feel time pass, yet the indentions and scars of ages on your hands told that time moved too fast.

Imagine when your last day of existence comes leaving you to realize that you're still in that same spot, and you have been there in the same location for so many years.

But yes, if you were to be asked to look back, you wouldn't be able to shut your eyes and know where each piece of your surrounding was located, because through life nothing ever stayed the same.

Everything was always moving, and maybe inside of you anger grew and feelings were born because you wanted your surroundings to change.

You wanted to be moved from that spot that you stood in as you lived the existence of this universe, but your feet grew tired, and you could not stand anymore.

All existence is gone now, and no longer are you standing in that same spot; now you hover in another existence, which is your grave.

Now no life lurks inside of you, and you are now deaf and diseased, but in that world that you left behind, you will always stand still in that spot because that is where your soul did die.

Ignored Laughter

They laughed at me—my goal was to succeed
Their laughter made my heart cry and plead
I thought this goal of mine was great
But to these people, it was fake
Should I also laugh at these dreams I call goals?
Or should I ignore the people, for they are fools?
I will succeed
And make these people believe
Years from now
I will stand in front of this same crowd
With great achievement and laugh them down
For I know now that I stand at mighty higher levels than this present
crowd

Immortal Mother

Shallow streams intertwine with hellish thorns
Vines divide the forest from twisted nature
Shadows cast mystery among brush
The sun closes its eyes and falls blindly behind curtains of nature
Now the night dwells with divine captivity
The fog casts demons from the swamps that dwell in an abyss of night
These are my dreams and this is what I imagine
Nightmares parade my brain as I sleep
When I awake I only just begin to live them

Innocence

Nights are quiet around here, always, during the summer. Everything and everyone is resting; the summer heat and picnics leave us satisfied and tired as the moon comes up to play.

Underneath a roof a woman lies awake not because she cannot sleep but because her heart sings a song of sorrow provoked by an unfortunate experience. Deep within her memories she holds his face with her hands, and for the first time she closes her eyes as in her memory she smiles at him and remembers the love in his eyes. And he then leans forward and rests his lip upon hers and in no hurry does he take them back. Tears swim in her eyes, and a love is born as it is placed in the arms of her heart. In a hurry, he wraps his arms around her and speaks words of security and trust. Inside she feels the breath of heaven give her permission to love him. Then fear tiptoes in and consumes this wonderful man. In her mind he becomes distant, but to have faith he screams at her.

Words are erased from her tongue, raging wave's crash down upon her, and with tiny whispers she cries out loud, "But I am not your weakness." A woman now closes her eyes in pain and to the heavens she sings a song of sorrow contained by an unfortunate experience.

Insecurity

In depth with insecurity
Pretty faces, skin of beauty
No reflection—me, just a stranger on a train car
Tracks break, step out and walk home
Cracked cold wind blisters me
Stop, a puddle, cold feet
Out loud a scream, insecurity
A death
She pulls me from a pocket
In me she sees no reflection
As a face reflected in the water, her heart reflects herself
Insecurity
She breaks me; I shatter
She smiles
A train car; she rides home
The window, a reflection
Only beauty, a proverb

Insomnia

Taken from in anger
I resent this thing
My poor and weak soul pours from my brain
The old wood soaks up this soul
The cracks drink it
It's out now, jumping on the planks of wood with fury
Scram now, it says; scream, for you are free
Courage, knowledge, love, jump from me now
Rebuke my ever being
Reawaken the woken
Bring home the lost to me
Recapitulate my soul to rest
Don't remark, soul
Fly now, reach for my strength
Rebellion feels me
Rebuke my ever being
My soul perambulates the wooden planks
It gasps
With all my voice I do speak and scream
I am together now
Come back to me, existence
I am ready now
To sleep

Invisible Castle

I cannot breathe in here, not here
Weary of this place, sleeping in this still air, eating, and even
attempting to cry
So alone
No movement, there is no movement but I, just me
What it would be like to see a face, smell something delicious, see
other colors than that of my own
Quiet, alone; dreams, though, keep me sane. Still, it would be nice.
All asleep, out of practice, my lungs, heart, and stomach
No air to breath or possession to love, I am hungry to
One window, one piece of light; no use, it does not even keep me
warm nor can I even lie within it
My favorites are wallflowers, silent music, and the feast that I pretend
to eat
Outside one word, one voice speaks to me; come, my old mouth repeats
Come get your wings. This is my chastisement; one day I will forgive
my impurities
In front of me, a key; it lies among my clothes. I prefer to cradle
myself naked
So easy to escape, but this is my self-captivity, self-punishment
A rose without a stem or soil to nap upon, hungry men with no
grounds to feed upon, the wind without any legs to run, a thirsty
tongue but no mouth to drink, how my soul relates
So, sweet world of make believe, touché, touché

Jigsaw

Weakened soul
I do cry
I am no soldier
Hero, I am not
Stop tugging on my sleeves
What do you want from me?
I am weak
I do doubt
Not proud of how I feel
My name, no glory
Dirtied path, burned black ash
Help me find
Help me seek
My mind and soul, a fragment
Lost fragment
This picture of mine is incomplete
Missing pieces makes a picture lose its value
This is my picture
Find the lost fragment
Jigsaw
This piece of the puzzle
Never taken out of the box

Ship Wreckage

The wind seems different today; it moves like it just borrowed something for a while and plans on returning it when it's done using it. And the day seems still, seems sad, and sits back in the corner as life and all its company has a delicious time.

The outside begins to carry the tune of the children and it forms a certain comfort inside of me. My doors and windows lie open.

My escape lies above the first floor and opens up unto the sky. A bunch of old tree limbs carry a story, and with the help of its leaves and old bark-like skin, it begins to read to me.

A drifter leaps down from the top of the roofs surrounding my escape and prances into my room, letting out a simple meow. This the cat says to me: "Life is so beautiful." We turn it ugly with our peer pressures and actions.

Failure, the loss of love, and betrayal can quiet your world. Rains will pour, clouds will darken, and the pounding of pain will ache in your heart with such force.

Your eyes begin to shower your face, and guilt cradles all you are. Life shuts up, and silence becomes your new true friend.

Eyes swollen, and the anger begins to dance with your sweet soul. Lost inside the fast train, open your eyes and take the right track.

Your body becomes hidden in sorrow. You are too far away for happiness to cradle your cries. But he loves me; his touch is what takes me away; he surrenders only to the beauty his eyes see.

I'm worth fighting for, yet I am the only one who can defeat him in his own battle of newfound glory. New existence; he sails on with his ship and I, his only treasure; he buries me deep inside the ground of his soul.

With wrong words that might hug my tongue I can cause a hurricane, and to the sea he will be gone. Sweet wind, sing me a song and just let me listen today; I'm not deaf.

A kiss of love makes a new king and me his queen. Then the wind blows; he tells me it's refreshing.

Jury, Set Me Free

Saddened now, life is not fair
Let me vanish, sulk in despair
Murder me now, is all that I think
Certain weapons and emotions are my link
Evil now sings with my depression
Look at me; I'm giving Satan an impression
How is the thought of me accepting evil funny?
My love for glory is as sweet as honey
I'm lost, trapped in an open sea
Waves keep drowning me; waters part, and people set me free
Pits and abyss have grown as a friend
Blackened flowers I now tend
Great gratifying glory, fill me once more with that glowing hope
My hands are faced upward; pitch me a rope

Just an Example

A grandson sitting in a pew only among a couple and a few
Eyes pointed forth as he watched his grandpa sing about the Lord
I couldn't help but notice the everlasting smile on that boy's face
As he watched his grandpa with such a godly grace
You don't have to always be working to get my chores done
Your wars with temptation will take place but I forgive with a loving grace
Just a simple, gracious, simple appreciation will do
Along with that quiet time full of I love you's
Grandson didn't have to be doing much and still that grandpa would
adore him with much love
Even after disobeying and times of doing wrong
Hanging out with temptation, giving in to a bad situation
Grandpa still looked at him with a loving touch
Church service ended and that grandpa and grandson stood laughing
I remember looking back with such an understanding
So I got down on my knees in front of that first pew
Praying God, Thank You
Thank you, God, Thank you
For showing me how to love you, to have mercy, and how to be true
Thank you, God, for showing me your kind of sweet love
Between that grandpa and grandson

Knight Rider

The night I ride, it is not blood that flows through my veins but spiders.
I am an illusion, shattered glass, reflection mine; it melts the mirror.
I keep you awake at night, the fear in your stomach: that is me,
puking; and the tears on your face: that is me, just spitting.
Crippling, isn't it; shredded flesh, bleeding innocence, an unlicensed
reaper.
Whisper, is it a secret? I can still hear you. Twisted hearts, what's
wrong? Are you feeling guilty? Of course not.
Graves' graves. I see your name. Blame, hate; I am that death under
your nails.
Seduction—it makes love to your lips, it feels good; rape, cut your
lips from your face; bury them under the dirt.
That is not sweat, you're drowning; maybe your sheets will create a
nice little necklace, a beautiful brand of suffocate.
Here is a shovel, some gloves; bury yourself. I have moved out just for
you.

Lifehood

I started out young
Verbs didn't even peek my tongue
Memories are faint
The smell of emotions set in the air like paint
Absent from my family at a month's time
Life was a blur; it was a crime
Reunited and loved again
Light now shunned in my darkened den
Childhood was rocky
People with attitude were cocky
Moved to a new area
Life switched and spread like malaria
Teen years were cold and hot
Family and friends were my resting spot
I felt good and hate
Life at times was hard to appreciate
My soul came out and I let it educate
Words poured from my soul and represented fate
Life was rough
Roads were tough
Love came thick
Now love is straight as a stick
I changed over the years
Swollen eyes are proof of tears
At times I hate what I became
Now I know that my ideas are tame
My past made me who I am
Life now holds me in its hands
Thank you, God, for I'm found
My soul escaped that selfish pound

My Literature Motive

Crouched in the mist of my shadow
A shadow that cast the image of an unopened gift
The ribbon that held the gift together began to shake
My eyes searched for the stranger whose hands were shaking my gift
A pariah I was no longer to the hidden gift inside of me
This stranger, my inspiration
The stranger's hands opened to me a skill, a technique, a gift
This gift did not sit beside me but in me
It was presented to my heart and not my mind
This stranger of literature opened up to me a box of emotion
Of Poetry
A beautiful mind she corrupted
This stranger, my literature motive

Living

I know when I'm running low
I know when I have to go
I know when I'm going to fall
Because I'm not living at all
Sometimes life's just that way
It makes you tired and then you sleep away your day
It gives you the pouring rain when you really want the sun
It gives you an empty pocket when you really need some income
Sometimes life's just that way
If I was to count my days
I might forget a few
Don't ask me how many times I won
Ask how many times I lost
Oh, I have lost all my patience
And I'm just living with a few
Now I'm just standing on this solid ground
I just got done falling
Maybe I'll just stay down
This just really makes me mad
I can't even walk
My days aren't light; they're just always dark
Well, I'm tired of counting my cards
Waiting for the sun to shine
Counting my last coins
I'm going to walk this line
And leave it behind
I'm going to stand next to life
I'm going to push on over
Scream a little louder
Here now is where I live

Location

Help me, please, sir?
My map is soiled
Useless now
Where do these roads go?
Thank you, sir
Streets with buildings
Filled with buildings
I know him
I know her
My car sits in park
City sounds
Scattered souls
Did they ask for directions also?

Lost

My head rests against my arm, and my eyes are glued to an open
space on my plastered bedroom wall.
Silent, no thoughts, and my brain is sleeping yet waiting for
something to sneak out and wake it up.
I don't know if that will happen, because even though air dances out
of my mouth, my soul sleeps in a coma.
My legs hang over this chair, and as they hang there I feel them
whispering to themselves, wondering why the carpeted floor looks so
far away.
My clothes are upon me, just resting there against my body.
My body, a function of time, like a great clock.
So empty and away I feel, from the existence of my location in reality.
Lost inside, I feel nothing but thoughts that aren't accounted for.
Confused, speechless; and a friend to the definition of pariah.
Hated I feel, but love I now have.
What shines through my eyes, I wish I could only see.
Such emotion and shadows lie within me to cover up the visible.
My bed is never made and the imprint of my body still remains in the
sheets.
Maybe that is where I left myself.
I am only a leaf that fell to the ground with the oncoming of autumn.
I am as a leaf, only a light weight, and expected to give a farewell to
the branches that I hung from. Not only did I change and become
at home on the ground, but also the branches changed and became
home to new buds.
The hair of the tree is no longer invisible to the wind of winter but
visible now with green leaves.
I am like that leaf, and I wonder if the brown of my old self would
stand out above the green leaves if I were to float back up to the
fingertips that once held me.

Lost Wars

I do not feel like walking today. My mind is crying from agony that has spread all throughout mankind.

The birds aren't singing today.

The storm must have scared the heart of those birds that sing.

My body has been clouded with emotions and sickness.

For this happening I do not blame the allies but humanity.

Throughout my body, my soul shakes.

But what, so strong, climbed upon me, and covered me with such feelings and emotions?

Was it the news that brought high counts of lost humans, lost to bullets or toxic air?

To what extent can I hang on any longer, for I no longer can act in faithful and happy action.

I am free of weapons or objects that kill, but in my heart I cry.

I pray for those across the waters fighting, and I try to live for those here at home.

Love

I miss our talks
Afraid to sleep, but his voice makes me feel safe
I can't see him
I long in agony for the moment that I will be able to
At times I feel so stupid, because love feels so corny
In all it's just a sweet emotion
He makes me laugh
When he is gone, I miss him
Things get said that are cruel and misguided
That's when I feel as if I have fallen in an abyss, alone
I wonder if he feels the same
I love this man
He has given love a name

Love Sent

New to the world of love was I
Scared to love, left to die
A stranger walked upon my soul
He created for me a love, a whole
Whispers and emotion is all he can be
His face and eyes I cannot see
Left to wonder the presence of he
His words and thoughts set me free
Alive and wonderful I now feel
My open wounds of love now heal
Who is this man to me?
To allow my body to sing sweet melodies
Angry emotions we sometimes show
Along with sad and happy foes
Where is he now?
Will I hear from him, how?
Our mixed emotions make me cry
I would take a sword, let me die
His soul is mine cut in half
Now we share an open path
Both a vision we do see
This man is a page of love to me
Fear is love and so it will be
Now knowing this, I know what love can be
No appearance can I engage
But our feelings of blind existence will not be betrayed
Miles away we are, apart
Our love will not grow less, because love has no address

Mask

Standing here on cracked soil
Frozen in time and too afraid to move
Time will stop and I will breathe
When no one is looking, I'm free
This mask I wear is taking away from me
My lungs rot and decay
My image fades into the atoms of air
Stop time so I can breathe
Human eyes and disappointed glares
Never failing is my burden to myself
Fake masks cover me
Hidden identity soaks me in protection
I'm dying here in my pretend
I don't want to die in a plastic mask
My face of flesh is scarred
Blinded eyes and weakened face
To have faith is to know
Time has stopped
Visible face and eyes that can see
I rise from this soil, and I breathe

Meadow

My family is a meadow
My dad is a tree
Standing tall and protecting us all
My mom is the grass
Green and beautiful, always being walked on
My sister is a flower, tall and petite
Rising tall to look best
I'm the meadow watching it rest
I keep it alive and together

Mother

Troubled by the windy paths she took
She passed the dollar and took a penny
No more do her eyes shine with the sunset
Between the eastern clouds but with rain
Evaporating with the sun into unknown existence
Many miles from home, but so close to family
A woman of many years, but a child at heart
So strong she is to me, my idol
Her soul dances within her tears as her past and future
Play poker for the winnings of emotions
Even though ropes hold her down, she is inexorable
And burns the knots of the ropes with the loving flame
And determination of her soul and heart
Life has not taken away the seed from her as she claims it has
But only has given her a can of water, which she is too weak to pour
upon herself
I choose to be her hands and let her not think God is ashamed of
her, but has only given her the sun; a seed's most desirable element,
oxygen
I pray for her to breathe and to no longer suffer from the limitations
of earth and soil, but to rise above the hardened ground and feed the
many birds that rest upon her stem

Muse

I was a still wind hibernating in the dark places of home
Sharing a place on the floor, watching the sun spy on my shadow
Turning an empty bottle, numb in thought
Breathing and moaning with hunger for something hot
I need to redeem, but only innocence screams
Awakened while slowly living through life, I stumbled
Close friends are skeletons who visit in the night
Moon keeps me close in light
Ravens watch over the graves and whisper to fly
Sleep, dear, and pray to keep warm
Dewdrops will wait for me in the morning to pass by
And fall will create a muse, and I will escape
With my love who meets me in color
The night is not silent, for the dead are in concert
Here at night I am not alone, nor can the dark become acquainted
with thee
The willow—she sings of a goodness, and the crosses whisper his name

Nature Dwellings

I want to be the misty wet dewdrops that soak the early morning earth.
I want to be the breath of the wind that chills the desert sand.
I want to be the sun to aid things in growth.
I want to play in the orchestra with the crickets.
I want to feed the bluebird.
I want to dwell with nature.

Attracted

Sweet porcelain is her beauty
Speaks loud
Let the blue abyss from up above gently paint your face
Her love, my captivity
No cages, just her sweet affection
Fingertips glide upon my face
Just as the water teases a thirsty tongue
Scream out loud, my lugs they cry
This is my surrender, my land, my way
Breathe just slow breaths
You left inside of me your murder
What is Egypt without its pyramids?
What am I without mine?
Just let the sun set and the dark skies keep me warm from this
coldness within my heart
A fool you are
Happiness surrounded you and buckets of love
What more did you want?
Afraid of yourself
Never too late

No Bondage

Caution tape consumes me; it rests in tangles around me, holding me
to this forest floor.
Age nestles on the surface of my skin.
I am now a part of this soil, and there is no one to hold me but the
roots of this neighboring pine.
To scream might get me found, but punishment took my voice away.
Rain falls in droplets made of stone, and not even the moon shed
enough light for me.
I could break free of this bondage but crime took my strength away.
Moans cry out from the pit in me, hungry.
Dew from the morning air nurses my thirsty tongue.
Abyss is where my memories sleep and even to my own heart I am a
pariah.
My conviction is sin, and my prison is this hell.
I have no expression; I own nothing, not even a face.

Noise

My inner self is yearning to scream
I can't take this sound anymore
The sound of verbal anger from mouths so sweet
Pique my highest level of tolerance
It impaled my veins and stampede its way into my heart
How could sound, a visible thing, lacerate my soul?
The sound is gone now; it has vanished now
My veins run with its normal blue
My heart beats with its normal rhythm
I can think now
The verbal anger from mouths so sweet sleeps
How can people create a sound so piercing and rude?
I can now hear the soft whispers dance from their mouths
It was war with them, but now they have surrendered
Why does peace sometimes have to be created by anger first?
An old adage I heard once before
With verbal speaking comes sound, which one may not want to wear

Outer Space

Life is a celestial fantasy with endless hopes
I wish at its stars while it glows with promises
Slowly, fully, the stars make my dreams realistic
And I keep wishing
Fantasy pounces upon my wishes and I smile
Suddenly it rotates and causes my mind to overcome the realistic
Then it wakes me up
Gives me back to my realistic location
And I realize I am standing on the celestial grounds of fantasy

Painting

Dry skin itches my body
My eyes peer out the open window
The leaves dance in the trees
Cats invite the birds down to play
The wind sings a happy tune, and nature is its orchestra
Above, the sun sits as a spotlight upon earth, so that the shadows of
myself can lie upon the ground
Sweet love prances the souls of the hopeless,
and Aphrodite plays her cards
Such beauty of all that live is only the makeup on reality's face
Our eyes do not fool us
Our hearts can really love
Our minds are not what trick us; it only is our emotions
But our fear is what makes us blind
To how we see the life, which we stay alive for;
life cannot be without me

Peace Offer

Trapped in the wake of a dream
Awake with the thoughts that haunt us, like a thousand moths
trapped in a lampshade trying to find a freedom that will only lead to
an end
Trapped impressions of my earlier age stay indented in my skull,
while shadows of vines suffocate my lungs
One form of home exists in this soul, so easily submerged in hollow
minds
The homeless crawl in through the windows
Society knocks on the door but I pretend I am not home
Peace made this deal
In the river I come clean
Tongue drinks and visitors sing
I place these hands over my face and peek between these fingers
Honor me no more, a plea
Great light from heaven pushes through to see me bleed
The bad blood; a sinner no more

Here I am

Here I sin
Here I am, on my knees again
Here I am, eyes closed shut and looking up
Praying, please
Here I am, and here I sin

Can I have my cross?
Yes, times were tough
Can I share your blood?
Yes, I give it all to you
Here I sin

Take my shoes and there I'll walk bare foot to foot
Take my hands and make them clean
Take my heart, soul, mind, and set me free
Take my prayer and hear my plea

Don't turn your face from me and hide
Don't reject but please accept
Don't close your heaven gates to me
Please, I pray, please, I pray

Let me walk, but only behind your footsteps
Let me share your love, but only with your love
Let me give, but only with your gift
Let me show, but only with your experience

Here I am
Here I sinned
Here I came to your loving hands
Here I give up all my pride and selfishness
Here I am, forgiven

I trust in you with all my heart
I don't depend on my own wisdom but only yours
I seek your will in all I do
I know you'll be there
This is what I want
Here I sin
Hear my prayers
Let me back in

Poet Mr. Hyde

Out from my heart and absent my own mind
I write
Words dance across the paper
Lines sing in anticipation
Breathe in deep and write
Formulations in alphabet create
Poet chemistry
Elements create a reaction
Secrets open their mouth
I tell on me when I breathe
These fingers stretch to touch their sky
Created is a breath to write
Oxygen by a poet
Now to document this in lab

Monday

Living, just living, is hard enough
Strength, well, that is just a joke.
Days they just come and go
Love, love makes me sleepy.
Today my eyes are dry.
Kindness is silent.
My eyes try to run away from my face so I will stay awake.
Do not think too deeply into what my words may mean.
For once just say nothing.
Sweetly lay here with me without my lips touching anything.
Dreams are lost as I close my eyes.
Ponders
What is life?
Is it a turning point?
A wrong way, gone astray?
Or is it atonement?
Is it a loathing word full of atrocity?
Can it be nice and gentle?
Paralyzing you in a state of law?
Or can people be so sweet like balm?
Or could life be a bauble?
Whose value is so little?
Whatever it may become, life is always questioned.

Priceless Souls

Candy-coated emotions fill my pockets with extra change that can only be spent on items I can't have. A demand I shout, and a demand I do not receive.

The soles are torn and my bare feet show against the soil of this earth. This earth that everyone despises and hates. This earth where people want and need.

These people who can't accept and thank. Selfish people roam this earth full of such greed and agony. These people upset me and these people make me sick. This earth is beauty and these people are parched offerings and not of any human form.

A bit of population glows through, and this bit of population consists of good people who accept and realize. Who is not too stupid to realize his own faults, and who doesn't mind learning from his mistakes these people are decent, and these people do not hate.

I wanted to run away, and I wanted the greedy to fall from the face of mother, but they wouldn't. It's bad for me to even think that way, so my intentions are to stay, to stay here, and to accept.

To be the leader and to help the lost. To change the greedy and to change the color. My candy-coated pocket of extra change will be put forth for the amount of human items I can't afford.

These souls I will save through the higher majesty that I came from. This is my war, and this is my victory.

Privilege

I have had the privilege of talking to this man
Yes, I have had the privilege of holding his hand
I have had the privilege of asking him his name
And yes I have had the privilege of becoming one of many saints
My feet have walked the soil where he was beaten down
My heart has shared his blood, in that church where I was found
My hands have grown blisters where I dropped my cross to the ground
My eyes have cried many tears, as they spit on this man's crown
I close my eyes and whisper a simple prayer aloud
And in my words I speak, I tell him I am proud
He didn't call those angels to take him from his cross
He didn't look upon his hands and hate his followers
Instead he looked upon his blood and across that great hill
With nothing but love for us and promise not from hell
This man gave us a choice to live not enflamed
But to rejoice in a kingdom, in a love where we're all the same
He lived, died, and was buried, and rose again on the third day
Only to take all our sins away
I know I have done my wrong and spit upon your name
But you're the only man that will love me through my shame
No, I can't keep going without this man; that I know
I love this man with all my heart, mind, and soul
Satan can't take me from his loving arms
I will eat his bread, speak his word, and share all his charm
I will ask for forgiveness and then through his mighty love
Through Jesus Christ above
I will feel quite precise
That I have had the privilege of knowing Jesus Christ

Prophet

His eyes are quick
Sudden flashes in the middle of the air
Eyes are speaking; I can hear them
So scared but free
Green fill his pupils
Such a pretty color
His Adam's apple moves under his skin
Some would say he is just swallowing
I know, though, that he is not
Tears he is keeping back
He is choking them down
Oh, such a sad creature
He moves his feet now to a more comfortable position
This ground is soft, and you can kneel upon it
On his knees now
He looks so dazed
I think he is embarrassed
It would be nice to help him
Your hands are not splinters; use them to shield your face, if it makes
you feel better
His hands hide his face now
Blue tears soak his skin
He looks so sinful
His black slacks crinkle with the movement of his shoes
I feel for him; let him grieve
Toward the sky now he does look
He has found me, my face
It is okay, little one; a prophet you now are

Proud

When I feel proud
I feel pink
When I rescue children from
The words of loathing
I feel proud

When I shut the window on
Friend's problems
I feel proud

When I'm proud I feel like I'm floating on cloud nine
The feedback of anger ceases
The wind carries a high tune and the breeze brings
It to a higher octave

Then the pride backfires
And turns to a downpour of blue
The blue that lives in the soul of a tear

You feel like a piece of dirt
That has been stepped on for many centuries
And is followed by decades to come

Reborn

Aboard the rock so stern
Across the field that sways unheard
Up the brown, solemn tree
Over the intersected branch that sings
Between the broken bark with temptation
Near my cocoon I made with creation
Into my cocoon that smells like honey
I look past the fields I am leaving
I waddle back into my cocoon and sleep
Throughout the fall, and I awake
Spread my wings against the wind
A beautiful butterfly reawakens

Redemption

Invincible by trade, we are hired
Chic in attire and starch perfume
Rich, paved aisles look up to the streetlights
Both giving direction
Winter winds mingle with your coat to tease with a shiver
Quiet nights are scarce and sing alone at the window
Busy lives with much attention
Truth is served with hesitation
Sorrow is experienced more by the population
All in fear of leaving without accreditation
Death doesn't have to see our faces,
He knows our names, and like a wolf in sheep's clothing he will call
us out
Unknowingly we will answer, and in a shallow, quiet, and innocent voice
Will breathe our last breath as our blood paints the dagger red
Turn up and smile, well fed
Be humble to the heavens
Reap not the world like a prison
Kiss the sun with passion, and love the highest mountain
A name for you is always given in faith

Reincarnation

Eyes cannot see. Pools within drown me; I do not scream.
The blind light that looms overhead guides home like a lighthouse beam.
Lost fields of insanity consume me; blood on my hands and even my
shadow cannot see.
I fear what is ahead, but that when I stop to breathe, I shall never
more fear the unknown.
Here then I stand still to dream, to die in thirst and hunger, to reap.
As I approach the murky edge of no return, gondolas of lost souls
hide their weary heads in shame.
These are not my neighbors, nor where I want to stay; did these souls
cause their pain, blind eyes?
I gave mine away. "I do not belong!" I cried in my mind. These
strangers I see seem not to fear me.
Stop. Wake up. Conviction hath seduced me.
Take me for what I am, guilty as this nightmare; betray, and speak up,
nothing.
Lady-in-waiting. My hands quiver in shame.
At the blind side of the sword, I found deep sorrow as I progressed in
my journey to self-deprivation.
I find you, my forever. Hunger.

Romeo

Love is what creates snow in winter
A river in spring
A cool wind in the summer
And engagement in the fall
Love turns me on
Love is truth and love is a cure
Within it is a medicine to ease every hungry sorrow
To patch the sores inside the heart
A hero to defeat all corruption in the darkest hours
Love is to be loved and will love
Love is sweet on the tongue and everlasting in the heart
Love is a joyous name and dances in color
Incomplete would I be without a little love
Love is the emotion of all emotions that we seek
Creation sings a song for this love
Darkness will be defeated with light, for in light is love
It is feared by corruption
Love is a war, a war, a sweet war
That always will and shall shake hands with our victory
Love is universal, and it is the wind in my hair
Correction without error and love is a healer
It is the first voice of fall
Love is a never-ending season
Love is simple, and I thank God for it all

Sacred Path

As the days grew, I began to wonder what I was feeling.
Regret? Anger?
Perhaps both, perhaps neither.
I stand here on this middle ground of unknown emotions.
The day grew to an end, and the skies pushed forth a shadow around me.
I began to walk back to that place that I hated so much.
I didn't want to, but I was obligated.
Why? What was keeping me there?
Maybe a secret, an abyss of lost memories that screams at me?
Am I deaf to the sound of its screams?
I can't run or hide; it's impossible!
I must face my pain and fight.
Fight? Fight for what?
My opponent seems invisible to me.
I feel him though, his breath upon my neck.
Show yourself, I scream.
Nothing. Silence.
Paranoia sweeps down upon me.
I begin to run, aimlessly.
I'm not thinking.
Panic.
Now I feel anger and regret all over again because I'm lost, without a home.
Where do I go now?
I don't recognize any of my surroundings
I hear a voice.

Salvation

Take your hands from over your eyes and place them next to your side
Don't be afraid, why do you hide?
The world: see how it runs, see how it speaks, and see how it hums
But you, my friend, you make this world live
Speak out loud, for the world is a mystery and you are its clue
Ages of unexplained life and how it goes
But you, yourself, help all begin to know
Like the rages of storm and the calls of the lost
You are the navigator, can life afford your cost
Do not feel fear of life itself
You're the secret key on that plain, high shelf
The world is dumb, don't you see?
The world reacts to how you are
It does not take magic or spells to defeat
It takes your heart, soul, mind to be complete
Mercy from the skies above
Allows you to push the shove
You, my friend, must scream out loud and jump aboard
The world is small to all you are; take your faith, and fight, O Lord

Saucer

My eyes flutter from the tears of salt that fall
The fingers on my hands shake from saddened emotions
My stomach dances to a rhythm of blues
The essence of myself fades from hidden guilt
My life's flame burns out as the wax builds too high
The saucer that held the flame broke, and it was my fault
My salty tears blocked vision; my fingers wouldn't stop shaking, and
my stomach danced too fast
It was me who broke the saucer when I tried to relight the candle

Saved in Return

He is a soul to me
One who is caught but breathes free
Appearance of him is unseen
His wondrous soul is so keen
Death and sorrow he did carry
Now his great heart lies silently weary
So lost was he
His identity was a melted key
My arms so empty
The ability to help, lain sleeping
Brought upon me, this soulful soul
Through years of hardship we both feel whole
Unforgotten emotions parade his presence
He sank to hell and rose with that glory essence
This connection rotates around my knowledge
Trapped endeavor now grows into a vine of foliage
Love we grew over years of war
This helped rebuild our saddened cores
Thank you, friend, and I do love you
Through rapture of hell and heaven we remain close
We remain a chapter

Savior

Splurge now
Drip from my wrists
It is this object that I hold that did this to me
Don't say I did
I didn't want it
Stop convicting me of a crime that I did not perform
This pain did it; this feeling in me reached out
Stop taking from me my life
Leave me alone
My name, what is my name?
I lost it along with my pride; now let me die
Don't cut that rope
Let it hang me
Don't try to talk me out of it
Why are you opening your hands to me?
I do not see anything
What are you trying to give me?
Hope

Secret Christ

High above the beds, a symbolic craft hangs on the papered or
plastered walls
Low on a shelf beside the bed, a book of religions and lessons lies
Resting in two hands, beads and a mother of the past are prayed upon
Tears fall down the face and speak of loss, the absence of a man, of
our brother
In my heart either fear or faith dwells, not to part the sea but to believe
Inside lies a man of unknown words but of actions of survival, love,
and sacrifice
Inside next to the man lies another, an enemy
Shine with the man of survival; love and sacrifice to fight the enemy
Invisible scars will lie in your wrists and feet but only when you look
at the symbolic
Craft, feel the beads, fight the enemy, and read the book of religions
and lessons
Most crave to believe and have a faith
I don't have to walk on water to feel faith but walking on ground with
my hands clasped
Facing toward the heavens, I speak in praise; it is a great beginning
All that lies under the water is ground anyway, just has an absence of
the water

Set Me Free

Time is a clock and at times it will just stop ticking
The time will die because you don't have a clock to tell you what time
it is
That would be like living in the dark surrounded by only a two-foot
area
I feel like that at times already
My life is like a broken clock in the dark and that only makes it worse
It's so quiet in the dark but the voice and nonstop noise running
through my head are like that of a busy subway
It's chaos and I'm so tired of it all
I now sit with a broken clock and a two-foot area with silver chains
tied to my wrist and affixed to the wall
I can't cry anymore or put pitiless expressions on my face
Instead of everything moving, I sit here paralyzed to the world
I care no longer what happens next; I'm just thinking about being free

Shakespeare

O sweet love, tickle at my toes, and cause me to laugh so hard I fall.
O sweet love, catch me, look there; your hands are so tired from
reading my body like Braille. Love causes you to be blind.
O sweet love, my cheeks grow bright with blush; laugh with me so I feel
not alone. Swept away by your gorgeous embrace, my eyes grow tired.
O sweet love, sing me a lullaby and cradle me asleep, and awake me
with the dawn of sun at my feet and with sweet berry juice on my lips
as you kiss me good morning. Take me into the rain.
O sweet love, dances with me, and whisper to me how I'm still so
beautiful with my hair in tangles and smeared eyes. Then graze my
nose with yours.
O sweet love, tease my mouth with an anticipated kiss. Slow
breathing, from our hearts beating, makes the raindrops like ice, but I
don't mind it because o sweet love, your mixed blue eyes heat me like
a furnace.
O sweet love, even in the rain the birds would sing. The rain is over
but you have created a storm within me and our eyes together create
the last few drops.
O sweet love, tickle at my heart, cause me to laugh so hard I fall.
O sweet love, catch me and carry me naked to the warm parts of your
heart.
O sweet love, embraces me, and sings to me a lullaby.

Silence Speaks

The quiet
The uncertainty of what is to be said
The dark
The light it tries to capture
The abyss of waiting to capture the thought of two
The tranquility, the faith, the deep end to solution
The question the mind ponders
The puzzle it puts together mentally
The answers, thought, and solution the fragile mind beholds
The waiting to see the other's reply
As the silence speaks

Sleepless In Seattle

Another night of endless sleeplessness.
Temptations and sorrows keep my eyes open, and worries are the
worst at tucking you in.
Love holds my heart at attention.
Thunder and rain sing too loud for a lullaby.
For what watches us at night that we sleep with closed eyes?
Mercy, I cry out.
Chains and straps are my blanket.
Self-esteem issues in my dreams.
Dawn, a new day, and here I am still awake.
With late morning my eyes close, and here I sleep with no
interruptions.
Comfort nurses my pillows.

Staff

Dances through the head of humans
Lifted, I am
The sound covers up the screams of anger
Free, rise now
Gone, glory sings within me
My existence inside of an amp on stage
My heart beats with the symbols
My body vibrates with the strings of the guitar
My soul shouts with that of the vocalist
My home and my security
Lyrics are my base
Summer
Open up your eyes now
Gaze at the horizon
Reach out and feel the sun set upon your fingertips
How it soaks in
Your veins are alive; the throbbing of the blood passing through you
Plays a musical flow against your mind
Open your hands now
The dew is falling
It has sweetened your lips
The coldness of the drops settles into the cracks of your lips
Moist on the skin of your face
Inhale now
The wind has carried in the scent of honey
The aroma feels your stomach and you feel hungry
The thought of honey fills your body with an appetite
Wake up now
Summer is leaving

Tame Me

Wide abyss crowds my thoughts.
Fingers with no prints kidnap my soul; their ransom is my life.
Creep across the hot earth, and all light must fade.
Yearn and cries echo from my soul.
Simpleton they are, and a fool they live.
Watch the skies rain from the sun and the moon fall with the stars.
My eyes sink back with my head.
I lie awake, ashamed, nude, and afraid.
Oh hear my plea, and let my heart be cleaned.
No worth have I?
True love does wait.
Anger tickles my soul.
He whispers to me, and through the expression on my face, he knows
he won.
Murdered and corrupted, wisdom stains me.
Save me; I fear his home.
Glory of your power I ignored.
Forgive me; I have fallen to the temptation of sin, O Lord.
I am a fool; a hungry wolf I became.
But with your love, I can be tamed.

The Others

The world is a very debatable environment. Some people's jobs are to debate what is good for the people and what is not. I grew up through life not ever knowing if I would be alive to watch the moon rise or if I would be too busy to notice the things that really matter in life. I have a lot of regret toward the decisions I have made and I wish I could turn back, but I can't. The world to me as I grew older began to scare me, and my fantasies of fairies and dollhouses began to fade. My dreams and play dolls began to take on an identity of reality. The world in my eyes was no longer fake, but as real as real could get. As a child you can see things in people, and it's almost like a power, only a power that walks with adolescence. Now, though unlike a child, I am still able to see; but now I can look into the eyes of a saint and relate to the goodness of his heart or I can look into the eyes of the accused and relate to his sins. I paraded myself with such happiness, that I was a good person, but as I grew older I realized much more that I had never even dreamed of wanting to know. The universe as a whole is huge and dynamic. I cry here on this earth because identities in a single soul are just strangers. Trust can no longer be held, because this world is growing. I feel fear, and I begin to doubt myself because I can see things. I know I am not alone, and as each day goes by I try to strengthen myself to be a shield against the nightmares and to be a warrior against the dark forces. The belief in the glory of God almighty is my army, and whether others agree in Christ is not an issue because this is I, and this is my fight. Visions of green grass turning to red fluids of tear my soul, and I scream in pain. Tears fall from my eyes and a sudden straight emotion overtakes my face. My eyes gaze through the hardened core and I straddle the crack in the core and all at once the world shifts. Anonymous choices start to speak and the clouds are turning with every color known to knowledge. The wind is hot and at times cold and the wind races underneath me. The grains of soil move slightly to the left and my opponent faces me with such an ugly face. No weapons in hand do we hold, but instead we fight fairly with the power of our souls and the strength of our body. My opponent, who I know oh so well, who tries to sneak into my heart every time my barrier to myself starts to fade, looks me in the eye. Myself and I have to fight, and the evil of a human, myself, will prevail, and this monster of myself will sleep in agony and rot in the pit of my existence. I no longer will live my days in a feeling of presentiment because now I have succeeded and my lack of feeling confident dies and vanishes. I could never doubt myself, no matter the lies that were cast upon me or the names that I was called that people found funny. I'm still strong and my body now stands like a stick of iridium. The times I chose good over bad I slash into my heart; the times a broken bone healed faster than I predicted, I wrapped around her body; and the time I cried the dark half of me but only to make her exist in hell with my faith and carved good into her sleeve. I'm free now and you see I am all ready to explore the inevitable. Chains will never bind my arms and cuffs will never encircle my ankles. You monster, you will now watch me kill off your ever-existing, sick, and abusive companions that provoke you, Lord, now to clean me of my other blood and to dress me in clean clothes. I never knew until now that I am more dangerous to myself than I am to others. Grounds are made to be fought on, but you're your own adversary.

The Pharaoh's Dance

Stay sweet and hold on, for the wind will soon be gone
With the morning the sun will rise
Ancient pharaohs and rulers again shall die
Beautiful open space takes the way
Tombs and stones built to stay
Years and years have gone away
At night the spirits of queens and pharaohs come out to dance
No, dance, sweet Egypt, and relive you old-aged days
Climb your mountains of sand and play
The wind will soon be gone
So dance fast now and sing your songs
With the morning the sun will rise
In your tombs your history will hide

Tired Eyes

Heavy breathing way too fast
Everything is just too real
My emotions lie to catch the sun on the windowsill
I try to wake up, I can't
I'm just way too stuck
Optical illusions fill my head
I can't count all the times I lay dead
So hard to open your eyes
I want to wake up from these dreamy skies
My heart breaks
Too many dreams my soul just can't take
I try to set my mind from the real, the fake
They just won't stop; they're just so real
I cry and scream to wake up from these dreams
Broken hearts, body ripped apart, happy endings, and witnessed
killing
Now I'm awake and about to break
I have to stay awake
No more dreams can I take
Tired eyes
Tired eyes

Twisted

Cold distortions intertwine with my fingers of youth to warrior. Humorous the world can be and immortal how the mortal can transact into. Sin so strong and evil so weak, too ironic to actually be. Cut in half this soiled core and let the dust fade into newborn grains. Paralysis takes effect and we freeze. Thinking too much causes migraines to scream and cry. So different everything claims us to be when actually we are alike and share a force so precious that being able to grasp it is a blink of un-happenings. Taking this world for granted and crying when one is not handed a wanted item. So foolish we are and so angry I am. Blind, so blind people can be. Take this, take this earth, and give to yourself everything. Seasons to pick from, flowers to grow from, animals to feed, and smiles to laugh. Do not wish for anything bigger and do not make yourself your own adversary of granite. Just stop bleeding from your pupils when the rich man sees gold. Scared of knowledge is what we are. Forgive me for being so angry. Hypocritical we all are, including the mouth that words of wisdom come from. Cry no more but just smile. Uneven planks above masses of water; there you shall go. Think and ponder about how the grass is green but how the rocks will be stained with your liquid if you choose to fall. Scared? I am. Don't you see them and can't you hear them? Thou shall choose between my shoulders. Without these and those I cannot survive and as much as I can create controversy amongst the other forms, I need them. Oxygen comes short, and I can only breathe so much. Just scream and cry. So tired and weak. Not you, do not create such a cuss against your own self. You, my friend, are my survival and my gift. Precious you are, and ugly shall not have a name. Here now is where we rest and close our eyes. The greatest shield against our armor of glory and nature. Slip into rest and dimension of medicine. I feel free and I'm so happy. You can see nothing but open blanks of air and the wind blows so softly against the open space. So white here and open to colors of pearls. I cannot feel the air or smell the odor. Such relief inside, I feel. So naked I feel and so angry at myself, I yell. A visitor appears and the bones inside my body began to fade. All I can do is cry, and so empty without words to describe, I keep crying. Heaven shall not judge my soul and myself with failure. So furious that I can't take the sins away from the sinners, and so upset I am that I can't feed all the hungry. Wake up people, wake up, and just look around. We are no longer becoming followers but survivors. Those will fall behind and it is you that stay strong. Gather forms of images and place them in the care of yourself. My knees meet the dirt and now my color is changed. So cold the tears are against my aged cheeks and such words of sorrow I speak. My skin is rough on my hands as I place them together and face upward towards the heavens. So sorry, Father, for I have sinned in my attempt to cure what I could not. Through acts of anger I have only become a hypocrite. Through you though, Father, I shall learn. Is it so wrong to seek your wisdom and power, Father? If so, strike me. My idol and leader, I worship. I only with old faith will remain as something that I already know. To you, Father, a child is born.

Under Heaven

Open fields are grey
Hell is pouring down
Flooded fields of red
Loud screams cause chaos
I'm drowning here in vain
Souls are burning and I lie awake
Trapped in cages of steel
Tortured soul alive; I'm yelling
Body limbs embedded inside
Sandy soil fills my gashes
Evil now does scream in anger
Let me out, oh, let me see
I'm holding on to nothing
Falling free into abyss
Life is faint, now ain't I?
My underworld is now in heaven
I am saved
Tears now soak this hardened ground
Nature seeps on through
Colors change to a faded gold
Immortality has taken over
Crossed on over to heaven, yes
No more cracked surface
Golden gates do now open
Am I dead or just now living?

Unknown

Confused and lost to all
My poetry to pose
Emotions and breakdowns
I have fallen down and gotten back up on the wrong feet
Sane into insane
Uncovered to covered
Led into a mystic cave
Walked out into the abyss
Take me away
Break me and abuse my bad side
Tears dance down my face
And soak my clothes, waiting for their applause
Cuts into my flesh red liquid matches the whiteness of my skin
Red and white colors of love
Disturbed, I am
Hand reaches out; grab me
Who am I? I am I
What do I look like? The reflections in the mirror
Essence pours out of me and now
I stand naked in holy water

Wall of Love

Hello, wall
Naked with morning dew
To you, wall, I will preach of love
Do you like being a wall?
You're just made of hard stone
Reminds me of love
People use you, wall, to separate their territories from others
Reminds me of love
You can't talk, people can only touch and feel you
Reminds me of love
You're firm and strong
Reminds me of love
With age, cracks will cover your face, wall
Do you remember me, wall?
I remember you
Look at all the age covering your face and the inside of your body
You're still standing with all that age
Reminds me of love
You must be standing on some precious ground, wall

Vagabond Dreams

Here I lay in the warmth of a Kleenex.
The cold crisp air dances with the naked trees from which fall stole
their clothes.
Shadows continue to stare at me as I press my bare back more firmly
against this weathered wall.
I no longer fear what may stare back.
Quiet; everything is at rest except me.
My eyes await the birth of the sun.
It is then I shall close my eyes, when I will cry in my vagabond dreams.